FROM THE HILLS OF INDIANA

TO THE SHORES OF CALIFORNIA:

LIFE AFTER AGE 60

Life experiences of people over 60

Compiled By

Geneva Shedd-Wright and Charlotte Gore

ISBN: 1-4140-3362-1 (e-book)
ISBN: 1-4140-3360-5 (Paperback)
ISBN: 1-4140-3361-3 (Dust Jacket)

Library of Congress Control Number: 2003098717

This book is printed on acid free paper.

Printed in the United States of America.
Bloomington, IN

1stBooks - rev. 02/16/04

Personalize this book.
Add a picture of yourself
or a friend here and a
descriptive statement
or message below.

_____

_____

_____

_____

_____

_____

This book is dedicated to our mother, Ruby Alice, and to the memory of our father, James Ivan, who through example taught us the value of hard work, a positive attitude, and humor. They taught us to laugh. (Appendix 1)

ABOUT THE AUTHORS

Charlotte Gore and Geneva Shedd-Wright are sisters. They are the second and third born in the Sluss family of five children. Geneva was born in 1940 and Charlotte was born three years later—in 1943.

In their former life adventure, Charlotte and her husband, Joe, resided in Northridge, California. She was a Human Resources Manager for a major national bank in Northridge and assured that equal opportunity was provided to all of the bank's employees. Recently, Charlotte and Joe demonstrated it is never too late to start a new life adventure. They recently traveled the U.S. collecting new life experiences.

Geneva resided in Bloomington, Indiana, with her husband until his death in October 1997. Until her retirement in 2001, she was the Director of Indiana's Bureau of Aging and In-Home Services. She administered a budget of more than $265 million per year and provided services to individuals age 60 and above and to individuals with disabilities of all ages who needed assistance in order to maintain their independence. During retirement she has enjoyed traveling, missionary work, building Habitat for Humanity Homes, visiting nursing home residents, church work, and other volunteer activities as a part of her new marriage to the Reverend Maurice Wright.

The two sisters were taught at an early age that all things are possible through hard work, a positive attitude and a sense of humor. They lived with such sayings as: "It is the little things that make a big difference"; "Anything is possible if you believe that it can be done"; "Anything worth doing is worth doing well"; "Together we can accomplish more than can be accomplished individually"; and "Good is not good enough if you can do better". Variations of these old-time sayings later became popular and were converted to works of art and placed on the walls of offices to inspire personnel.

As the sisters approached age forty, friends started making reference to the big 40—in a joking way. They did not feel any different and could still do the things they could do at age 20 and age 30 so why was all of this attention being given to becoming age 40? Charlotte stopped telling people her age, and Geneva decided to submit an article on "Becoming

Forty" to a major magazine and both sisters were shocked at the response. This shock was converted to a passion to dispel the attitude that age limits what can be accomplished.

It is with this passion that they scanned magazines, newspapers, and other publications for more than eighteen years to spot articles on the many valuable contributions of individuals of all ages with a focus on age 60 and beyond. This book was written in an attempt to share the sisters' findings during those years. It is not intended to be a research document, but rather a document that highlights the contributions of individuals age 60 and above and the fact that their contributions appear in major publications in the United States on a regular basis. This book intends to educate and inspire people of all ages.

For example, during just a few weeks (in the summer of 1994, winter of 1995, and a two-week period starting in March 24, 1996) at least one positive article concerning individuals age 60 and above appeared in major newspapers and magazines the sisters read each day—some publications had multiple articles. (Endnote # 1)

From 1994-1996, the individuals highlighted in this book created a moment in history that serve as an example to us all. No attempt has been made to follow these individuals through the ensuing years. The authors maintain that whether any of the individuals continue to achieve greatness does not impact the moment that they were highlighted in national publications.

CONTENTS

INTRODUCTION

It started in 1979. And what is it? "It" is the passion to write this book about the wonders of life with a focus on age 60 and beyond.

Life was good for the two sisters who authored this book. In 1979, Charlotte was a successful businesswoman who was employed as a Graphic Arts Manager by a major real estate consulting firm while freelancing as a graphic artist. Her photographs and layouts appeared in a number of publications that were widely read by individuals interested in emerging trends in real estate. She had traveled extensively and had developed an interest in capturing the facial features of people from different climates and different cultures in her photographs. Her black and white photographs of buildings and landscapes appeared in publications and were framed for display in special showings. After settling in California, she had a dream of someday writing a book and including some of her artwork in the publication.

Geneva was an administrator who had succeeded in what had been called a "man's profession" of

Deputy State Director of Vocational and Technical Education in the State of Indiana. Few women occupied this position in the United States at that time. Her achievements were featured in national publications under titles including "Women Take Leadership Role in Vocational Education"; "To Be an Administrator, and A Woman"; and "Strengthening the Role of Women in Vocational Education Leadership Positions". Her work on State and National Boards and Commissions resulted in numerous articles and papers being published in professional journals. She was eager to be published in a national magazine outside of her chosen profession.

As the two women approached 40 years of age, Geneva wrote an article and Charlotte edited it for possible publication in a well-known national fashion magazine. The manuscript, on "Becoming Forty", was about the joys and anxieties of approaching age forty. This educational and entertaining article ended by stating that "Age probably has never been any good as an index to people, but a lot of emphasis has certainly been placed on it."

The manuscript was mailed to the magazine in New York City on March 27, 1980. The sisters celebrated. A response was received less than two weeks later. What a disappointment! The five-paragraph form letter dated April 9, 1980 stated "I'm sorry I cannot answer your letter personally, but I do hope this letter helps you understand why we were unable to accept your Viewpoint. Again, thank you for your interest…" in our magazine. The magazine's Editor signed the letter.

The Editor <u>did</u> respond to the letter personally. She wrote a personal note at the bottom of the page that read: "P.S. I'm sorry, but very few of our readers are 40. This topic is inappropriate for us." (See Appendix 2 for a copy of the letter)

This came as a shock to the sisters as they both read the magazine and believed the magazine was ignoring the interests of a large group of its aging readers. The authors felt discarded by the magazine because of their age, and they no longer subscribed to it. This narrow approach that left out the majority of the population was not in keeping with their philosophy of being glamorous by being in tune with one's body, mind, and emotions regardless of age.

This rude awakening from this national fashion magazine caused the authors to be even more sensitive to the aging process and to the wonders of life, regardless of a person's age. It created a passion to learn about people of all ages. For more than eighteen years the authors have collected information about the talents and contributions of people from the hills of Indiana to the shores of California.

Both of the authors are now over the age of **60**. Through this book, they are sharing the information that they have learned about people—people age 60 and beyond.

The sisters enjoy gathering with their Red Hat group. It started as a small group of four, but today has grown to include family and friends of many ages.

More Red Hat friends!

TO BOB, WHO INSPIRED US ALL

He was a good man, an honest man, a tough man, a gentle man, and he was kind.

Even in his final days of life when people came to help him, his last words were, "Can I do anything for you?"

It is sometimes a struggle to recognize that as physical beings, we are not going to live forever no matter how much we try, how much we love, or how much money we spend. But, Bob's memory will live forever in the hearts of the many people who knew him and loved him.

The profits from this book will be donated to the American Cancer Society in his memory.

PART ONE

EIGHTEEN YEARS
OF READING, CLIPPING, SORTING
AND
FILING

People of all ages in Bloomington, Indiana, including Sally Wegener and Clay Ludlow above, contributed to the Experiencing Place: The Evergreen Project Journal. The journal focused on discussions about their environment and what was important in their lives.

AGE IS NOT A GOOD INDEX OF PEOPLE

Eighteen years of reading, clipping, sorting and filing articles about people of all ages confirmed that age is not a good index of people. It also confirmed that individuals of all ages have talents and make contributions to life, to their community, to their State and to our Nation. This chapter focuses on what the authors learned about individuals of age 60 and above.

Individuals age 60 and above, like individuals below 60, do the following:

VETERANS

Some are veterans of the U.S. armed forces; some are not.

CREATIVITY, WORK AND VOLUNTEER SERVICES

Some work full-time, some part-time, and still others are retired. Some volunteer their services to help others; some do not.

PHYSICAL FITNESS, RECREATIONAL ACTIVITIES, AND HOBBIES

Some participate in physical fitness and recreational activities; some do not. Some have hobbies; some do not. Some like to shop; and some do not. Some travel; some do not. Some give advice; some do not. Some have relationships; some do not.

GRANDPARENTS AS PARENTS

Some are parents to young children, others have grown children, and others have never been parents. Still others are "parenting" their grandchildren or other children.

Ninety percent of those over 65 live quite independently in their own homes and communities outside an institutional setting; 5 percent reside in long term health care facilities; and another 5 percent live outside an institutional setting with the assistance of others. The fastest-growing age group in the United States is age 100 and beyond—the centenarians.

FOURTEEN CONSECUTIVE DAYS OF POSITIVE PRESS

During a two week period starting March 24, 1996 at least one positive article concerning individuals age 60 and above appeared in major newspapers that were read by the authors each day. (Endnote # 2) Articles were on the subjects of:

Cook Device on "ER"! The intraosseous infusion needle manufactured by Cook, Inc. in Bloomington, Indiana will be used on an upcoming "ER" show on NBC. This special medical device is used in certain pediatric emergency cases. The needle is an alternative for physicians when access to normal blood vessels is impossible because of injury or trauma. Cook, Inc. is the world's largest privately held medical device manufacturing company. William A. Cook, age 60 plus, is founder of Cook Inc. and President of Cook Group. Other Cook Group companies include: Cook Urological, Cook Imaging, Monroe Financial and CFC, a real estate company. Cook Inc. grew from making catheters in a spare bedroom in 1963 to an empire of 48 companies employing 3,000 people worldwide in 1996.

Music is IU Dean's Life, Future! The Indiana University School of Music was named by U.S. News and World Report's annual Best Graduate Schools Guidebook as the country's best music school, an honor it shares with New York's Juillard School and Rochester's Eastman School of Music. The three also tied for the honor in 1995. Charles Webb, Dean of the I.U. School of Music, was age 64 at that time.

Staying Behind the Wheel! George Ross, 93, waves to friends as he leaves Crestwood Village Apartments for his daily trip to the store in his 1985 Oldsmobile. Ed Schneider, 83, just likes to tool around on four wheels. He drives Downtown almost daily to the Indianapolis, Indiana Senior Center. Ross and Schneider are among more than 24 million Americans over 65 who regularly drive, according to the National Safety Council. Betty Hall, 78, thinks any policy that keeps older drivers on the road is the correct one. She drove for decades in Northern California.

Whitney Houston Always Thanks Aunt Bae When Accepting An Award! Who is Aunt Bae? When Whitney was growing up, her mother was often on the road performing. Her mother's best friend, "Bae" frequently cared for Whitney and her two brothers. Aunt Bae now helps to care for Bobbi Kristina, 3, the daughter of Whitney and her husband, singer Bobby Brown. Aunt Bae is age 60 plus.

Job Finders: Co-Directors of Nonprofit South Austin Job Referral Service in Chicago Finds Jobs for Residents of All Ages! Age means experience, which surely counts in the workplace as value added.

Evergreen Journal a Recommended Read! A new publication, Experiencing Place: The Evergreen Project Journal is 89 pages of writings by young and older people in Bloomington, Indiana. The journal gives two often under-represented groups a voice. The writers were invited to discuss their environment and what is important in their lives. They do just that.

Marriage For The Ages! He's 103 and she's 90. One Friday, they sealed their wedding vows with a kiss. About 250 people gathered in the Chapel for the ceremony. They had lived in adjoining apartments and began spending a lot of time together. "People were beginning to talk and we wanted to avoid a scandal." They will now share an apartment and pretty much go about their business. As the old saying goes, you're only as old as you feel. "I haven't felt this good in a long, long time," said the new husband. They are hoping for a long and happy life together.

Bedford Man Happy to be a Veteran of War and Life! Brooks Anderson of Bedford, Indiana, is the first veteran in Lawrence County to receive a 50-year VFW membership pin. Anderson will celebrate his 91st birthday in October of 1996. "I've had a good life", says Anderson. "I sent all six of my kids to college and they did really good," he said. "That's something that is important to me." If he had it to do all over again, there is little he would change about his life. "I'd do it all again, including joining the Army," Anderson says. "I was proud to serve my country."

At 73, Indy Woman Pursues her South Pacific Mission! She plans to stay there for at least three years. I can't wait to get there, she said.

Carl Stokes, Black Political Pioneer, Dies of Cancer at 68! Carl Stokes was praised as a pioneer whose election as mayor of Cleveland 29 years ago was a political watershed for minorities. He "was a lifelong role model, not only for African-Americans, but for all citizens who share his abiding concern for his fellow man," Governor George Voinovich said. Stokes, appointed ambassador to the Seychelles Islands in 1994 by President Clinton, took a medical leave from that post in the Indian Ocean last June after his cancer was diagnosed. Clinton said Stokes was a friend and valued colleague who "brought energy and humor to every task he undertook".

High Court Makes it Easier to Win Cases of Age Discrimination! James O'Connor took his age-discrimination case to the U.S. Supreme Court when he was fired by a coin catering company. The Court rules unanimously that employers who fire workers over 40 and replace them with significantly younger people may be breaking the law even if the new employees also are over 40—someone who is 60 is fired and a person of age 50 takes the job. While the decision only means O'Connor's case will return to a North Carolina federal court, the opinion indicates that corporate America cannot hide behind the age of a replacement worker to avoid a charge of discrimination said O'Connor's lawyer.

Center Helps Arthritis Sufferers Maintain Limber Limbs! Under the leadership of Bobby Smith, who is certified through the Arthritis Foundation, people who have arthritis can exercise at a pace that suits their needs. The land-based arthritis exercise classes "strengthen the muscles and relieves stiffness of the joints," says one participant. A number of aqua aerobics classes are available for people with arthritis, but only a few land-based exercise classes are taught.

Ameritech's Contributions an Effective Marketing Tool! Betty J. Williams of Bloomington is featured in an Ameritech marketing campaign launched in March 1996. Called "Giving Back: Ameritech's Report to the Community," the 20-page booklet cites various examples of Ameritech's community involvement in the areas of community service, corporate contributions and economic development. Williams is shown at the City of Bloomington's Older Americans Center surfing the Internet by computer, which was installed with the help of a $10,000 contribution from Ameritech.

Museum Pays Tribute to Best Little Marketing Tool in the Business! House of Cards: Founder

Ken Erdman, age 70, is a marketer and collector who founded the Business Card Museum. Erdman has a collection of 156,000 standout cards. He has cards with photographs, die-cut cards, heat-sensitive cards that change colors, cards made of glass, leather, wood, and china. "The business card is probably the least expensive and most often used form of advertising. It is kind of an extension of yourself." Geoffrey B.W. Little, Sydney, Australia's smiling policeman has taken law enforcement to new heights by passing out cards with his grinning likeness and the words: "Smile, you're under arrest!"

Proof Positive! Muncie photographer Ruth Chin is still leaving her prints on Indiana journalism. When she was 9 years old, Ruth Chin took up a hobby that would become her life's passion. With the help of a neighbor boy, Chin ran a photo processing "lab." Her friend would go door to door in the Muncie, Indiana neighborhood, picking up film for her to develop and print. "We had our own little business," says Chin, 71. "Some kids sold lemonade. We sold pictures." As the owner of Ruth Chin Photography, the first-generation Chinese-American does advertising, corporate and aerial photography. She has been writing a photography column, Positives and Negatives, for the Muncie Star for more than 30 years.

Additional positive articles featuring individuals age 60 and above appeared in the newspapers that the authors read during that two- week period. (Endnote # 3) The selection of a particular article for this publication was not meant to isolate or idolize the individual described in the article. Instead the articles selected serve merely as samples of the activities and achievements of <u>all</u> individuals over 60.

PART TWO

WHAT THEY DID! WHY THEY DID IT!
AND
HOW THEY ARE LIVING LIFE TO THE
FULLEST!

Brooks Anderson of Bedford, Indiana was the first
veteran in Lawrence County to receive a 50-year
VFW membership at the age of 90. Anderson
shared his philosophy that guided him over some
bumpy times— "Keep busy, walk for exercise,
throw away those cigarettes and chewing tobacco,
and do your best each day." He maintained a strong
faith in the Lord, a healthy diet and a belief that life
is what you make it.

A SALUTE TO VETERANS OF THE U.S. ARMED FORCES

This chapter is a salute to the men and women of all ages who have served in our nation's armed forces.

Figures from the Department of Veterans Affairs reveal that people age 65 and above represent a whopping 37 percent of the veteran population.

This is what some of our veterans had to say:

In December of 1917, Horace Dobbs left his Southern Indiana home to answer his country's call to help fight World War I. He used the "don't ask, don't tell" rule when it came to his age. Nobody asked and he didn't tell that he was only 15 at the time. At age 91, he joined others on November 11, 1993 as they relived their wartime memories at the Veterans Day ceremonies which marked the 75th anniversary of the signing of the armistice to end World War I—to end what was once called "the war to end all wars." I wanted to be adventuresome and to get out and see the world, Dobbs said. His commitment to the Navy took

Dobbs to such faraway places as France, Iraq and Nigeria. (Endnote # 4)

Daniel Eugene Carmon, a young black man born in tiny Dixon Springs, Tennessee was a recent graduate of Fisk University, a traditionally black college in Nashville. He had made a deposit on his tuition, the University of Chicago had accepted him for graduate study, and nothing — not anything — could keep him away. He was on his way to the University when he found his name included in a long list of names in the daily newspaper. "Drafted," read the headlines. War takes lives and changes lives. He never made it to the University of Chicago. At age 101, he joined other World War I veterans across the nation to commemorate the signing of the armistice on November 11, 1918, that ended World War I. He wore his 75th anniversary medal in recognition of his service to his country with pride. (Endnote # 5)

Robert Purkiss, drafted out of his native Pittsburgh, was trained as a truck driver. Purkiss, an engineering draftsman and inventor by trade was stationed in Brest, the seaside town in farwestern France. His job was to shuttle supplies back and forth to the troops in the trucks he had learned to drive. "World War I was ugly even by the usual standards of war," he said. Much of the fighting was done at close quarters from trenches, each side taking or holding on to land a few feet at a time. Poison gas was frequently used. Purkiss was injured in the war and returned home on a hospital ship. He was age 100 when he received the 75th anniversary medal in recognition of his service to his country. (Endnote # 6)

World War I veteran John Hamlin, 99, posed for a portrait in Navy whites in November 1993 in recognition of the 75th anniversary of the armistice signing to end World War I. Memories are still fresh for Hamlin, who enlisted in the Navy because "I knew I had to go serve my country and do my duty." (Endnote # 7)

41 Tough, Crusty Paratroopers Re-Enact Their D-Day Jumps: What did Bill Coleman, Elsworth Hargen, Rollie Duff, Earl Draper, Ed Manley, Everett Hall and 35 other veterans have in common? They were among the 41 World War II Veterans ages 68 to 83 who leaped from World War II-vintage planes on Sunday, June 5, 1994 and parachuted onto French soil, just as they did 50 years ago. These paratroopers, described as "still tough, softened only by devotion to lost comrades", were watched by hundreds of friends, relatives, President Clinton, heads of states from 14 other countries, and thousands of others who gathered to commemorate the fifty year anniversary of the D-Day landings in Normandy. Each received a round of applause as they hit the ground. They impressed everyone and they certainly humbled old age. (Endnote # 8)

What were they thinking as they jumped? Most of the 41 pumped up vets—ranging from their late 60s to early 80s described the jump as a piece of cake, despite the shifting winds and their advanced years. (Endnote #9)

Bill Coleman, 70, of Orlando, Florida, had this to say— "What was I thinking? I was thinking this parachute better open up because this is the last jump I'm ever going to make." But I was also thinking of my old friends, the guys who didn't make it." (Endnote # 10)

Ed Manley, 72, of Briney Breezes, Florida, jumped wearing an American flag patch on his right arm, a special armband on his left. On that band were the names of his closest friends, all killed in combat, his personal roll call of honor. (Endnote # 11)

Harold Rice, Danny Thomas and Hal Veenker, Marines who fought for Iwo Jima more than 50 years ago, were reunited at Purdue University during the summer of 1996. "We're close, it's more than brothers," said Hal Veenker. "We know what we did," he said "There's a respect we have for each other and a love we have for each other. I guess it sounds strange for a bunch of old Marines to say they love each other, but we do." On the morning of February 19, 1945, there were 220 members of Company C making their way to shores of Iwo Jima. Fewer than 20 of them were still fighting when the 24-day battle for the island ended. "We have a very strong bond," Veenker said. We kid and josh back and forth, but we don't talk about the war much. It's just hard to describe what this is like." They didn't realize then that the battle would be so prominent in history. But they know now. (Endnote # 12)

In October of 1997, a memorial was dedicated outside Washington D.C. honoring the nearly 2 million women who served in the armed forces — during peace and war — dating to the American Revolution. A Hall of Honor commemorates women killed or captured in the line of duty. Women's military contributions were never more vital than during World War II when some 400,000 women filled a manpower shortage and helped turn the tide for the allies.

Few history books tell about a woman named Deborah Sampson who fought in the Revolutionary War. She treated her own combat wounds to keep her secret but was discharged when a doctor discovered she was a woman. Today, more than 13% of America's active duty personnel are women. (Endnote # 13)

We did whatever it took, said Greencastle, Indiana resident Helen Hurst who survived German air raids while serving in North Africa in World War II. We counted tank parts, deciphered enemy codes, tended to the sick and dying and more. She recalls taking cover during nightly raids by the German Luftwaffe. "You had a job to do, and it was my country" Hurst said of her service. "You wanted to do your best." (Endnote # 13)

It's been more than 54 years since Elizabeth Dale, age 75 signed up for the Navy in World War II, yet she still beams about her experience and her pride in the servicewomen's memorial in Arlington National Cemetery. (Endnote # 13)

Comments from other age 60 plus veterans include the following:

Brooks Anderson, of Bedford, Indiana was the first veteran in Lawrence County to receive a 50-year VFW membership pin at the age of 90. Anderson shares his philosophy that has guided him over some bumpy times— "keep busy, walk for exercise, throw away those cigarettes and chewing tobacco, and do your best each day." A strong faith in the Lord, a healthy diet and a belief that life is only what you make it have gotten him through close to a century of life. (Endnote # 14)

She stood 5 feet tall and weighed just over 70 pounds. But her tiny build did not prevent Betty Taylor from enlisting in the Marine Corps as soon as she reached the required age. A half-century and 11 children later, Taylor still holds fond memories of her time spent as a clerk typist and machinist during World War II. "So many of us came home and hung up our uniform and went about with their private lives." She said. My uniform is 57 years old, but I still have it and I am proud of it." She is hoping other female veterans will dust off their uniforms and be recognized for their contributions (Endnote # 15)

Nearly 75 years after helping veterans of the first World War as a nurse, Ernestine Godfrey was honored in recognition of her service to her country. Ernestine enlisted as a second lieutenant in the Army nurse's corps at the Walter Reed Hospital in Washington, D.C. on June 17, 1920. "I wanted to be a nurse all of my life. I loved every minute of it. I just enjoyed taking care of people," Ernestine says. A fit 93, Ernestine still walks the three or four blocks to downtown Niles when she needs something. (Endnote # 16)

Vernon Baker waited for 50 years to receive his nation's top military honor for heroism under fire. The 77 year old retired career Army officer was a member of the Army's all-black 92nd Infantry, called the Buffalo Division. Although 1.7 million blacks served in World War II, they did not receive a single one of the 432 Medals of Honor awarded. He received his Medal of Honor at a White House ceremony in January of 1997, making him the first and only living black man to receive it for service in World War II. Six other black soldiers were awarded the Medal of Honor posthumously.

Harold Bennington was a rifleman with the 116th Infantry Regiment of the 29th Division. He says on D-Day the sky was black with planes and they yelled at them, "Give'em hell" —because they didn't expect to make it. They had been told that two out of three of them would not be coming home. (Endnote # 17)

Warren Rulien was a private with the 16th Regiment, 1st Division. As they got nearer to the shore, German bullets began hitting the sides of the landing craft. The ramp was lowered, and he stepped into the water up to his chest. He lost his balance and dropped his rifle. There were mines in the water and he pushed a floating dead body in the water in front of him to protect himself from the mines. Waves of soldiers were bunching up on shore and taking shelter behind a three-foot high seawall. They were being slaughtered. (Endnote # 17)

Ralph Goranson was a captain with the 2nd Ranger Battalion. His company landed at the western end of Omaha with about a thousand feet of beach separating them from an 80 foot cliff. He lost 23 men in the first half-hour, about a third of his company. As they climbed the cliff, the Germans were shooting them off the ropes as they climbed. (Endnote # 17)

Paul Jarrett, 99, was a member of the 42nd Infantry Division, later known as the Rainbow Division. He was the first man of his regiment to set foot on French soil in November 1917. He fought in the Battle of Champagne in 1918 and often had to crawl all night to capture prisoners. In 1918, an artillery shell blew him over an embankment and he broke his knee. (Endnote # 18)

They answered our country's call for help. Many put their lives on the line to preserve the freedom we enjoy today. They did what it took. Today, veterans are some of the most enthusiastic volunteers, selflessly giving their time and energy to do whatever it takes to help others. We can learn from this spirit of giving.

The Reverend Maurice Wright, 76, a practicing American Baptist Minister, educator, artist and devotee to community service officiating at an outdoor wedding.

A SALUTE TO VOLUNTEER SERVICES, CREATIVITY, AND WORK

VOLUNTEER SERVICES

Many individuals age 60 and above will continue to work full or part time, seasonally or year-round, self-employed or as employees. Some want to retire and spend time learning, growing and doing things for others. And still others want to do it all—work, learn, grow, and volunteer. As a result, networks of lifelong education and volunteer services abound.

Everyone who volunteers seems to do so for a slightly different reason. Volunteer opportunities appear to be limited only by imagination. Following are just a few of the ways that individuals age 60 and above are getting involved in helping others right in their own neighborhoods:

Seniors are very much a focus of both the outreach and volunteer efforts of many zoos. For example, about a third of the Indianapolis Zoo's 400 volunteers are age 60 and above; some are in their late 70s and early 80s.

Volunteer tutor programs are evolving in Juvenile Detention Centers in many States. Retired teachers and professors are a valuable resource in tutoring youth that are preparing for their General Education Diplomas. Tutors are finding that they are viewed as far more than a resource for math and other subjects. These volunteer tutors are often approached by their students for help in overcoming behavior problems and personal hurdles.

Seniors are vital to the health of many communities. They serve as volunteer "grandmothers" and "grandfathers" to the neighborhood kids. They volunteer as the welcomers, arbiters and organizers all rolled into one. They are organizing volunteer neighborhood crime watch programs and serving as the Crime Watch block captains. They tutor elementary students. They are often the "glue" that holds sometimes fragile communities together.

Mable was 93 when she died—on Easter Sunday. For 13 years she called to talk to the local newspaper editor. She gave advice. She gave words of wisdom and she shared her philosophy. She cherished common sense. "The secret of life is knowing what you can live without." "The key to life is what we teach our children and how we treat them." "You never know what a society is going to get all worked up about. Look at Vanna White."

Lynda Ayers, 60, lives in Bedrock, Colorado, and volunteers her time and stamps to answer letters from Flintstone fans. It started when a local postmaster gave her a letter addressed to Chamber of Commerce, Bedrock. (Endnote # 19)

Other individuals age 60 and above are volunteering in a variety of ways:

Tracking of peregrine falcons, an Indiana endangered species; logged more than 1,700 hours monitoring a pair of falcons and their four chicks nesting on Monument circle in downtown Indianapolis — age 68 (Endnote # 20)

Using storytelling skills to teach about nature — age 66

Retired math teacher keeps talent sharp by volunteering to **teach trigonometry** to peers — age 60 plus (exact age not given)

Portraying Santa Claus for past 50 years (since age 19) — age 69

Working at public school bookstore and supply store, and helps kids with their schoolwork, primarily math but other subjects, too. Most importantly perhaps, he talks to the kids — age 66

Serving as escort for new reporters, photographers and filmmakers; answers public affairs office telephones; and guides visitors and tourists around Kennedy Space Center for National Aeronautics and Space Administration (NASA) — age 81

Care giving for the elderly (providing relief for 79-year-old man who provides 24-hours-a-day care for his wife who has Alzheimer's disease) — age 68

Library volunteer finds joy lending children a helping hand as they come in to browse, read, work on computers or learn mathematical tables — age 82

Working as a **volunteer in the emergency room** in a major hospital making sure that people get to the right place at the right time — age 84

Serving between 50 and 120 meals a day to homeless people as a volunteer in a local care center — age 73

Retired electricians **creating "the world's tallest Christmas tree"** at the Soldiers and Sailors Monument on the Circle in downtown Indianapolis. The decorations include more than 4,600 lights — age 60 plus; exact ages not given.

Volunteering two days each week to assist in **making patients' stays in the hospital a little more pleasant** by wheeling her cart of candy, snacks, magazines and newspapers to a total of 168 rooms on six floors — age 98

Seniors **volunteering to make dolls** of muslin or percale and fill them with polyester for use by Doctors to help explain surgical procedures to young patients at the Children's Hospital — ages 60 plus

Raising funds for community projects — age 79

Serving as Security Officer in low-income housing project — age 92 (was buried with his badge of honor that was presented to him a month prior to his death).

Collecting and selling cans to give money to charity — age 69

Serving as a volunteer **firefighter** — age 78

Mother Teresa said that we don't need to go to India to help; we can begin right in our own neighborhood. There are many shut-ins who would love a friendly visit, a trip to the store, even a phone call. The above individuals and others are doing just that.

CREATIVITY

Can creativity evolve with aging? According to research into fields as varied as neurology, behavioral science and art history the answer is yes. (Endnote # 21)

There are numerous examples of older people exuding creativity throughout their lives—Picasso experimenting with new styles of painting in his 90s, Verdi composing new operas in his 80s, George Bernard Shaw writing new plays in his 90s. Thousands of famous and "not so famous" people turn to creative endeavors to bring new zest to their world of work and volunteer activities at age 60 and above. Others continue with endeavors that shadow those of their earlier years.

Alfred Eisenstaedt's unerring eye has brought our world into sharper focus. His famous 1945 photograph of a jubilant sailor planting a kiss on an unsuspecting nurse on V-J Day has indeed immortalized the fabled Life magazine photographer. Yet this is only one of countless familiar images taken by Eisenstaedt during a 70-year career. In 1993, at age 94 he was still practicing his craft. As his 95th birthday approached, Eisenstaedt was often on the other side of the lens. He was an obliging subject. Posing for a visitor, he gently instructed: "Move over there, where the light is better." Then he swiveled his hat around catcher-style and grinned at the camera. (Endnote # 22)

Gordon Parks urges youths to overcome barriers and focus on ambitious goals. Homelessness, poverty, racism and other barriers can't stop a person determined to reach his or her goals, says one man who ought to know. Gordon Parks, age 81, has faced each of those obstacles—and more— during his lifetime. But he has overcome them all. "If you want to be somebody, you have to dream," said Parks, a celebrated photographer, musician, composer, historian, essayist, film maker, poet, author and publisher. "And you can't put limits on your dream. You can't let anybody tell you that you can't do this or you can't do that," Parks said. Parks has been described as sort of the dean of black photojournalists. Parks, wrote the introduction to the 214-piece book collection titled Songs of My People-African-Americans: A Self-Portrait, a photo essay of mostly ordinary people taken by 50 black photographers across the country in 1990. "You can do anything you want to do if you first apply yourself efficiently," he said. Although Parks didn't graduate from high school, he has received more than 50 honorary college degrees. And though he has never had a formal piano lesson, he is an accomplished pianist, having played his first concerto in Paris. (Endnote # 23)

To her neighbors and friends, Connie Mason, a 63-year-old grandmother, is best known for her prowess at duplicate bridge and line dancing. For millions of strangers, Mason is their passport to exotic worlds filled with passion, adventure and romance. Mason is a top writer for Leisure Books with 21 novels to her credit. She is in the upper echelon of romance writers and has a strong following. Mason now commands between $40,000 and $50,000 per title from her publisher. She has about 2 million books in print, with some in their second or third edition. Mason doesn't plan on ever unplugging her word processor. "It's a thrill to see a new book come out. It's a real ego trip," she said. (Endnote # 24)

Sy Rosenwasser, 69, urologist-turned-sculptor creates sensual masses of bronze laced with his feelings about relationships. He has shown pieces in galleries in the U.S. and abroad. (Endnote # 25)

Norma Lyon, 65, says butter is just wonderful to work with, and last summer she sculpted a life-size, 400-pound likeness of Garth Brooks at the Iowa State Fair in Des Moines. Working mostly with just her hands, Lyon spent three days on the piece. Lyon has been making butter sculptures for 35 years. She states that Garth Brooks was about as hard as the Mamie Eisenhower that she did for the 1990 Kansas State Fair. (Endnote # 26)

66 year old Ernest Steingold of Burbank began decorating his van with brass ornaments after he bought it in 1978. The decorations now include a 20-pound brass eagle, 100 brass unicorns and winged horses, 20 life-size masks and 300 belt buckles. He owns Dreese Vacuum in Burbank, California. (Endnote # 27)

Alvin Straight, 73, paid his brother Henry a visit after Henry suffered a stroke. Since Alvin didn't have a driver's license, he fired up his Ariens riding mower and hopped aboard for the 325-mile trek. He hauled a 10-foot trailer to carry gas, food and camping equipment, but his mower broke down after just two days. He returned home and bought a 1966 John Deere lawn tractor and began again. During the next six weeks, he replaced his drive belt twice and spent $250 for new parts. So sore was he from the ride he was barely able to walk when he arrived. (Endnote # 28)

Charles Mosley, owner of Mid-City Salt Service, was 84 in 1996. He believed the longevity of his business was attributable to providing good service and believing the customer was always right.

WORK

Although workers age 60 and above are in the minority at this time, this group of workers is not dwindling. On the contrary, the numbers are quietly rising. Experts on aging and demographics expect the numbers of later-life workers to continue increasing as the 76 million baby-boom generation ages. (Endnote # 29)

In a world where small companies come and go, some continue as a Family Business. Mid-City Salt Service, Inc.'s owner carries on the legacy begun by his grandfather. It's just a small brick and cinder-block building with an office in front and storage space in back. But if you want to get a lesson in the history of Indianapolis black business community, this would be a good place to start. Owned by Charles Mosley, who turned 84 in 1996, the company is probably the oldest minority business in Indianapolis that's still in the hands of its founding family. "I don't see any need of retiring, as long as you're able to get around," he said. The key to the longevity of his business is customer service: "Give them good service and the customer's are always right" (Endnote # 30)

Hallie Stillwell has been a teacher, a cowgirl, a newspaper columnist, a storekeeper and a justice of peace. There's one thing she has never done: Sit and do nothing. And, she's not planning to start. You could see that she was pleased with herself after officiating at yet another wedding at age 97. Her portrait along with 35 others made up an exhibit at the Smithsonian, "Going Strong! Older Americans on the Job." (Endnote # 31)

The "Beardstown Ladies" —the financially savvy investment club featured in the national bestseller "The Beardstown Ladies' Common-Sense Investment Guide—hail from Beardstown, Illinois. Their first book sold more than 300,000 copies and was on the New York Times bestseller list for nearly three months. The Ladies, many in their 70s, have spun more of their straightforward financial advise and folksy attitude adjustments into a second book that focuses on the three R's of "risk, reward and return." Although much of the Beardstown Ladies' second book addresses retirement, readers who need to save cash for a new home or college tuition can also benefit. So far, the club's book-writing ventures have not brought in more profits than the investment club, but one thing is for sure, "life in Beardstown has certainly changed." (Endnote # 32)

On November 19, 1996, NASA's oldest shuttle soared into orbit carrying the oldest person ever to fly in space, 61 year old Story Musgrave. He broke the age record held by former astronaut Vance Brand, who was 59 when he flew in space in 1990. Musgrave also became the first person to fly six times on the space shuttles. Only one other person, moonwalker John Young, has flown so many times in space. John Glenn, the world's oldest astronaut at age 76 is preparing to rocket away on shuttle Discovery at age 77. He will be 16 years older than anyone who has flown in space. (Endnote # 33)

Eleven years ago, when William Schumacher wanted to be a Catholic priest, he wrote to 49 bishops asking for a chance. Some said outright that he was too old. One wrote that he would only get sick and be a drag on the diocese. Many didn't bother to answer the letter. With each rejection, Schumacher remembered a lesson he and his wife had taught their six children prior to her death. "If you know you're right, don't give up." He completed his seminary degree and was ordained a priest 20 days from his 80th birthday, and believes he is the oldest American to be ordained a Catholic priest. At age 87 people of all ages "flock around him" to say thanks for all the blessings and special services he has delivered. Extra chairs often have to be brought in to accommodate the large crowds. (Endnote # 34)

At age 87, Geneva Eberhardt still makes her Avon makeup rounds. She's been doing it for 50 years. Some of her family have suggested that she retire, but Eberhardt's not budging. "I quit when I die," she said. She has about 75 customers of all ages and races, and "they all worship their makeup," she said with a laugh. She's still a customer herself. (Endnote # 35)

At age 81, Joel McLendon works a 10-hour day. It starts at 7:30 a.m. in his company's Dallas Trade Mart showroom and usually ends with a couple of hours at home poring over blueprints at the dining room table. McLendon Company, co-owned by McLendon and his son, represents about 90 manufacturers of cookware and gourmet food items. "I'm having too much fun to stop," said McLendon. (Endnote # 36)

Evelyn Pitschke just retired after nearly half a century as an attorney. Variously referred to—usually fondly—as "feisty," "a mean, tough lawyer," or "a bulldog," the 73-year-old Pitschke is renowned in local divorce courts. She could (and may) write a book about her experiences. Her advice to today's high school senior is: "Expect to earn what you get." She is most proud of: "My reputation for fairness and being a survivor." Her most prized possession is: "My freedom—personally, and as an American." (Endnote # 37)

Jobs Program Helps Old Hands Stay Productive Longer. Henry Peshell, 90, spends 20 hours a week plucking staples from police reports for minimum wage, and hopes to keep working until he is 106. Even at 90 years I don't want to retire, because people who stop working die within six months. (Endnote # 38)

Herman Feifel, 78, has been a prolific writer, and his writings have changed our way of thinking about death. He emphasizes living each day as a beginning and stressing the gift of life given anew each morning after waking from sleep. He states that understanding that dying is not only a medical affair but also a human one. That life is not just a matter of length but of depth and quality. Healing the spirit is as important as healing the body. Though losing his sight, he states he is in transition and has a lot of fire left. (Endnote # 39)

Ely Callaway, 75, is an unerring thinker with a lifelong gift for dreaming the unconceived. First textiles, then wine, and now golf. He helped introduce quality clothiers to blended fabrics that looked good, cost less, and lasted longer. He set his 150-acre vineyard facing a coastal saddle where others maintained fine grapes would never flourish. For Callaway, that was the point. When the grapes grew, the wine was different than other grapes. Next he stumbled on a four-man company fumbling to stay alive making steel-core, hickory-shaft golf clubs and bought the company. The clubs are easier to play with and make the game more fun. (Endnote # 40)

Fueled by the desire to be everything his family was not, Warren Bennis created a world full of power and prestige. But now the business guru is wrestling with thoughts of fun. At 69, he has dated Ann Landers, been quoted by Al Gore and received faxes from the Dalai Lama. In 1994, he was one of the hottest gurus on the corporate consulting and lecture circuit, and says he is addicted to new experiences and ideas. (Endnote # 41)

79-year-old James Allen Murphey, Princeton, Illinois, for 50 years has searched the world for obscure long-dicontinued patterns for dinner-table china, has 16 rooms of china and annual sales between $100,000 and $500,000. (Endnote # 42)

Sam Maloof is known in the region and the world for his woodworking furniture. Furniture companies are eager to mass-produce his designs, but with the help of three assistants he chips away at his 500-order waiting list. Admirers from Presidents to Nobel laureates drop by virtually every day. His home is a testament to how you can live in a meaningful way by being true to yourself. Most major art museums have now displayed his work. (Endnote # 43)

George Burnham, 80, has 150 tons-of-rocks and minerals. He doesn't have a particular favorite, he likes them all. He enjoys picking up what most people think is an ordinary rock knowing that it's really something much, much more. (Footnote # 44)

74-year-old Pat Warner of Manhattan Beach, California, started her career as a foster mother 38 years ago. She has cared for over 189 babies that stay about 3 months, some only overnight. Pat believes love is the vital ingredient in the first months of a human life. (Endnote # 45)

Eugene, 66, and Carolyn, 65, Shoemaker spotted and were among the first to report the comet later named Shoemaker-Levy 9. Carolyn self-trained in astronomy holds the world record in comet discoveries. Carolyn's skill at scanning telescopic pictures for the tiny irregular light patterns that signify comets was key in making the identification. (Endnote # 46)

William M. Gray, 79, is one of the world's leading long-term hurricane forecasters, teaches meteorology and forecasting at Colorado State Univeristy, and predicts how many hurricanes will develop in a given year in the Atlantic and Caribbean. (Endnote # 47)

Dr. Alf Wight, 77, pen name of James Herriot practiced as a veterinarian author in North Yorkshire. (Endnote # 48)

Ineze Caston's, gospel choir director, goal for her choir to sing with one voice, feeling the same thing at the same moment and radiating what she thinks is the most important thing in life: love. (Ineze asked that her age not be printed.) She says senior citizens are the most resourceful people in the world. They have gotten through it. Her father used to say it takes more muscles to frown than to smile. She brings out the love in people. (Endnote # 49)

George Yellich, 67, a mortgage banker plays banjo every Wednesday evening at Skoby's restaurant. George is bandleader and gets to pick the music, orchestrate it and make tapes of his arrangements so other members can learn the tunes by ear. (Endnote # 50)

On weekends, visitors to Moe Di Sesso's ranch can bid or barter for everything from handmade Native American Crafts to used wet suits. Those with more serious business in mind can watch his pig play the piano. Most of his time is spent working as Hollywood's oldest active animal trainer. (Endnote # 51)

At 65, news correspondent and reporter Murray Fromson embarks on a new career as director of

University of Southern California's journalism school. He believes journalism knows what news is and what it's not, but objective reporters are a myth. Fairness and balance is what a journalist is about. Everyone has a point of view. A good journalist has to be a student of history. (Footnote #52)

Following are still more jobs the authors read about that were held by individuals age 60 and above. Many take the view that "I enjoy it and have no intention of quitting":

Actor/Actress - ages 61, 62, 63, 64
Artist - ages 80 and 102
Author - ages 69, 83, 87, and 90
Author-Veterinarian - age 77
Barber - age 84
Beautician - age 72
Carpenter - age 70
Cellist - age 72
Chairman of Airline - age 65
Correspondent - age 60
Custodian - age 60
Dance Instructor - age 70
Dean of Music Department - age 64
Deliver Packages and Letters - age 65
Deliver Prescriptions - age 74

Dentist - age 70
Dog Groomer - age 60 plus 67, 68, 69, and 100
Elementary School Teacher - age 79
Emeritus Professor of Physics - age 100
Entrepreneur, owns 2 dress shops - age 90
Farmer - ages 73, 94
Finder of Discontinued China Patterns - age 79
Fire-Rescue Unit - age 92
Food Restaurant - age 78
Foster Mom - age 74
Founder of Museum - age 70
Founder/President, Manufacturing Company - age 60 plus
Greeter, Major Discount Store - age 60 plus
Grocery Store Owner and Operator - age 72
Gymnastics School - age 60 plus
International Music Star - age 90
Lawyer - age 106
Magician - age 65
Maitre d' - age 108
Maker/Wrapper of Candies - age 96
Manages Toy Manufacturing Company - age 78
Marketing Consultant - age 95
Minister — age 77
Mows Greens and Fairways at Golf Course - age 65
Music Teacher - age 75

Needles Manufacturing Company - average age 73

Nurse - age 60 plus

Operates Bike Shop (sells and repairs) - age 60 plus

Painter - age 88

Pet-Sitting and Care for Seniors - age 77

Photographer - age 71, 88 and 94

Physician - age 80 and 85

Pilot and Flight Instructor - age 70+

Playwright - age 76 and 81

Poetry Therapist - age 75

Prepares Salads at Fast Food Restaurant - age 77

President/Medical Device Manufacturing - age 60 plus

Produce Department, Major Grocery Chain - age 79

Produces Gospel Radio Show - age 87

Proof-Reader - age 100

Realtor - age 80

Refrigeration Engineer over 78 years

Researcher - age 62

Restores Vintage Cars for Museum - age 63

Runs Own Laundry Business - age 101

Secretary - age 60 plus

Senator - age 94

Surgeon - age 80

U.S. Pianist - age 94
Waitress - age 74

Ken Dychtwald, in his book, Age Wave, predicts that we will see increasing numbers of older people working in a variety of service positions. Examples of these positions include security guards, hotel clerks, receptionists, limousine drivers, baby-sitters and nannies, small-company consultants, airline reservation agents, exercise instructors, media advisors, insurance-claims adjusters, travel consultants and tour directors, adventure guides, political lobbyists, editors, researchers, adult-education teachers, landscape artists, handymen/women, hobby advisors, and interior decorators. (Endnote # 53)

Employers are enthusiastic about older workers who find wage earning a lifelong habit. They appreciate their experience, reliability and work ethic. Many are retired from other careers. Some need the extra income and others just like the social interaction. Whatever the reason, older workers are filling lots of niches in the workforce.

Clair M. Duckham, age 91, rode in the 30th Annual
Hilly Hundred in Bloomington, Indiana and
surrounding towns. The 1997 "Hilly" was
Duckham's fifth. Approximately 5,000 Hilly
participants ride 50 miles each day of the 2-day
event.

PHYSICAL FITNESS, RECREATIONAL ACTIVITIES, AND HOBBIES

People today are living longer. How do we live those extra years in good health? How do we add years to our life and how do we add life to those years?

In reading about particular individuals 60 and beyond, the authors found there is an emphasis on improving the quality as well as the quantity of life. They found that healthier lifestyles save millions of dollars each year in health care costs. They found that exercise is an important part of fitness programs undertaken by individuals age 60 and above, and that variety is important in order to improve cardiovascular endurance, muscle strength, muscular endurance and flexibility.

In addition to exercise, proper nutrition, weight control, intellectual alertness, emotional stability, and safety are important parts of a healthy lifestyle.

Active seniors are involved in bicycling, weight lifting (pumping iron), running, walking, line dancing, ballroom dancing, track and field events, softball, horseshoes, badminton, tennis, basketball, swimming, yoga and more. They have hobbies, they shop and they travel. They participate in recreational activities for physical fitness and for fun.

Read on for additional information on how seniors are adding fitness activities to their lives.

PHYSICAL FITNESS

Youth vs. Experience—This unique Southern California tennis tournament recently celebrated its 10th year and remains a favorite of youngsters and seniors alike. Dodo Cheney, age 81 and the winner of 288 gold balls, and her opponent 10-year-old Cosmina Ciobanu attracted a large crowd at this fund tournament pitting seniors, some in their 80s, against the sections' top-ranked juniors, ages 10 to 14. It's a test of spunk and stamina against savvy and gamesmanship. There's no doubt that both sides benefit from this unique and colorful event. The kids love it. It's the most popular event that they run in Southern California according to Jim Hillman, director of Southern California Tennis Association junior tennis. Even though Cosmina won this particular match, the seniors got back on track with the biggest victory margin ever and now lead the series. Perhaps experience is the best teacher. (Endnote # 54)

John Ellis, 63, using a wheelchair and David Olsan, 62, an investment adviser stricken with polio at 25 are still fly-fishing. They are able to pursue their love for fly-fishing because of Joan Stoliar. Joan sixty-something initiated and Arthur Stoliar, 67, volunteered to carve switchback paths so individuals with disabilities could reach water to fish. Project Access was started in 1986. (Endnote # 55)

Nolan Bay, age 66, rides a high-wheel bicycle. The cycle is that fascinating contraption with a huge front wheel and a tiny rear one that makes you wonder how a rider mounts and dismounts. Bay is from the West Coast and recently attended a National meeting in Indianapolis, Indiana to recreate a national high-wheel bicycle meeting held there 100 years ago. Bay didn't ride all the way from the West Coast—only 500 miles from Springfield, Missouri. But 14 years ago, when he was age 52, he rode his high wheel from San Francisco to Boston. (Endnote # 56)

In San Diego, the Senior Women's Basketball league members range from age 50 to 81. Strong, healthy and athletic, these women are the epitome of '90s "girl power". They sport the latest in athletic gear, and their strong, muscular legs propel them on rebounds and jump shots. "Go ahead, tell them they shoot like girls. These women will take that as a compliment. They're likely to dribble past you, fake left, fire a sly pass and finish with a hook shot". This program began in 1993 when David Hall, director of the San Diego Senior Sports Festival, returned from the National Senior Olympics and noted there were no women basketball players from San Diego, and they have been playing ever since. (Endnote # 57)

A woman, age 81, told Ann Landers she was still interested in sex. This came as no surprise to Ann. She receives letters on sexuality from adults of all ages, including age 80 and above. (Endnote # 58)

Variety, many say, is the spice of life. This well-known adage holds true for an increasing number of seniors participating in the diverse fitness activities the authors read about. Read on for additional information on fitness activities in which seniors participate:

76-years of age — three days a week swims 1,000 meters at the local YMCA. On alternate days, she walks a mile and a half at a fast clip, and follows this warm-up with either a rousing game of volleyball or an hour of yoga. Other YMCA fitness programs include weight lifting, group exercise programs, indoor cycling, and more.

Record-setting runner Anne Clarke, has just begun to slow down at age 87. She's recently sworn off marathons, and does a 13-minute mile—a mile or two off her peak. But trim and toned, wearing bright blue spandex leggings and well-worn running shoes, the 87-year of age Clarke says she has no immediate plans to ditch her sport.

Since her first competition, a 10K (6.2 miles) contest she ran in 69 minutes, the same year she began the sport at age 69, Clarke has competed in more than 500 races worldwide. She holds more than 30 age-related running records in races from 5Ks to 26.2 mile marathons. From Finland to Hawaii, she has competed in eight marathons—her last in 5:54:10 at age 81 in Chicago, setting a national and world record for her age group. (Endnote # 59)

Clair M. Duckham, age 91, rode in the 30th Annual Hilly Hundred in Bloomington, Indiana and surrounding towns. The 1997 "Hilly" was Duckham's fifth. Approximately 5000 Hilly participants ride 50 miles each day of the 2-day event. Duckham was described by other participants as a spry, 91 years young participant that many guessed to be a healthy and active 70-year-old. (Endnote # 60)

Weight Lifting—A 1994 Study involving 100 men and women backs up the maxim that it's never too late. Extra strength can improve the lives of people in their late 80s and 90s, the Study said. Researchers dedicated the Study to their oldest volunteer, a former dentist who pumped iron for four years until he died at age 101. The researchers found that frail nursing home residents in their 80s and 90s got around faster, climbed stairs better and sometimes even were able to swap their walkers for canes. The results of the Study suggest that a healthier aging process can be achieved, but only by working at it, Deputy Editor Dr. Edward W. Campion said in an editorial in the New England

Journal of Medicine, which published the research. (Endnote # 61)

Senior Games held in many States include over 90 different sports including track and field event (including a triathlon), badminton, fishing, skeeball, running, darts, race walking, horseshoes, air rifle, shuffle-board, swimming, softball pitching, bicycling and more. Many seniors see the Senior Games as an opportunity to participate in games they missed out on as a youngster while others see them as a continuation of previous interests.

The key to any fitness activity is to have a good time, keep moving, and be positive about what you are doing. Speaking of fun, read on for information about recreational activities and hobbies.

RECREATIONAL ACTIVITIES AND HOBBIES

Activities the authors read about included everything from table tennis to bungee jumping to making an airplane and more. Following are a few of the popular recreational activities and hobbies of individuals age 60 and above:

Bicycling
Building an Airplane
Bungee Jumping
Canoeing and Hiking
Fishing
Gardening (Vegetables and Flowers)
Horseshoe Pitching
Horseback Riding
Inventing
Listening to Big Band Music and Dancing
Making Bird Houses for Others in the Community
Motorcycling
Novel, Poetry Writing
Oil Painting
Participating in Elderhostel Programs
Piloting Around the World
Playing Golf and Teaching Golf
Playing in a Handbell Choir
Playing Music

Playing Table Tennis
Playing Tennis and Teaching Tennis
Practicing Karate
Preparing for/Participating in the Alaskan Iditarod
Sail Boating
Shopping
Skating
Skiing (Snow and Water)
Writing Mystery Books, Romance
Telling Stories
Traveling (Sometimes with grandchildren)
Wood Carving

GRANDPARENTS AND PARENTS

While many seniors continue to work full or part-time, others enjoy retirement, and still others are serving as parents to their grandchildren.

According to the U.S. Bureau of Census some 3.7 million children live in a household headed by a grandparent. In fact, for almost 1.3 million children, a grandparent, often the grandmother, is their primary caregiver. The reasons for caring for their grandchildren ranged from teen pregnancies, parental substance abuse, child abuse, neglect or abandonment to incarceration, unemployment, divorce, and the death of one or both parents. Grandparents who take on parental roles often face a range of challenges including:

- lack of support and respite services
- lack of affordable housing
- lack of access to medical care
- lack of resources; living on a limited budget

Commitment to the youngsters invariably wins out when grandparents are faced with the challenge of becoming "second time around parents". Too many times the only other alternative is for the child to go into a foster home and the grandparents "come to the rescue." In some cases, however, the grandparent may use their life savings, or deplete their retirement funds to care for their grandchild. There is a growing network nationwide of grandparent support groups and many grandparents are turning grief and heartache into advocacy and action in order to pass laws to assist with this growing challenge in our Nation.

In August 1991, she agreed to raise her brother's three adolescent children. Liz Carpenter, 71, has written three books; one on "Unplanned Parenthood: The Confessions of a Seventy-something Surrogate Mother". She managed with humor, grit, and a lot of help from her friends. Liz states that "If there is any lesson I have learned, it is to express love. Every bit of love you can express is casting your bread upon the water—it will come back." (Endnote 62)

Mike Dyer, 62, travels the United States with his wife in a motor home. The excitement of the new sights and sounds he experiences every day are multiplied by the fascinating people he has met along the way.

ADVICE AND HINTS

This is the first time in history that we have had so many people actively living into their later years. And what we are learning from them is what science has been telling us for years: Chronological age does not have to be a barrier to productivity, growth or creativity. In closing this Chapter, the authors give some advice and hints that come from what they have read:

- Love yourself and love others.
- Take care of yourself and take care of others.
- Good nutrition and exercise are important parts of healthful living.
- Take advantage of your age and experience in your day to day activities, and share your experience with others.
- Relationships are important—family, friends and others; keep connected to those important to you.
- Everyone must have a dream, regardless of age. (What are your dreams?)
- Be productive.
- Be creative.
- Keep your mind and body active, regardless of your abilities.

- Listen.
- Take charge of your health; ask questions when you visit a Doctor; understand the benefits of any medication that you are taking and know any possible side effects of these medications.
- Be all that you can be and reach for what you want to be.
- Choose a lifestyle that is right for you.
- Be enthusiastic about life and living.
- Have faith.
- Laugh.
- Hug a friend.
- Count your blessings.

Geneva Shedd-Wright and Charlotte Gore

PART THREE

YOU'RE NEVER TOO OLD

Ione Auer, philanthropist and centenarian, is a music lover, drives herself on errands around town, and enjoys her independence.

THE FASTEST-GROWING AGE GROUP IN THE UNITED STATES: CENTENARIANS

The number of people in the United States who live to the age of 100 and beyond—the centenarians—has doubled every decade since 1970. This is the fastest growing age group not only in this country, but also throughout the industrialized world. There are more than 50,000 centenarians in America today. This growth challenges us to rethink what we thought we knew about life.

Willard Scott, the NBC-TV weatherman, started celebrating 100-year birthdays on the air in 1981. Instead of the trickle of centenarian letters he received at first, he now gets 400 a week. If Willard now wanted to send birthday wishes to every American who is 100 or older, he'd have to send more than 200 greetings every weekday. (Endnote # 63)

WHO ARE THE CENTENARIANS?

The lights burned late in the mountaintop studio of Ojai, California where Beatrice Wood created the works of art to be displayed in galleries and museums around the world. She is best known for her pottery, but her latest show offered drawings. Wood was 102 years of age. (Endnote # 64)

In a small, weather-beaten house in Eatonton, Georgia, Ida Eubanks displayed the dozens of jars of peaches and pears she had canned in the last month. Eubanks was 108 years of age (Endnote # 65)

At age 100, Audrey Stubbart was a proofreader and columnist who worked a 40-hour week at "The Examiner" in Independence, Missouri. (Endnote # 66)

Max Zimmer came to the United States from Austria in 1911. He was 18, and all he had was a $2 bill. At age 102, Zimmer still carried that same $2 bill—but he also had built a multi-million dollar business based in Los Angeles and given $5 million to charity. (Endnote # 67)

At age 106, John Morton-Finney was a logical choice to conclude the 1996 Black History Month lecture series "From Dreams to Visions: History of a People Explained, Expressed, Experienced and Explored." Morton-Finney was the oldest practicing lawyer in Indiana at that time. The black lawyer, born to a free woman and a man who had been a slave, told the group of black law students at the Indiana University School of Law in Indianapolis that like their ancestors, they could be successful in influencing the path of America. While proud and confident, he barely mentioned the successes of his own life in his presentation on other blacks in Indiana. For example, he had five law degrees, 11 bachelor's degrees, was fluent in 6 languages, and a successful lawyer for more than 60 years. A horse-drawn caisson seemed the appropriate way to transport John Morton-Finney, Indiana's oldest veteran, to his final resting-place on January 31, 1998. He was hailed as an Indiana legend, a national treasure, and a person of unequaled credentials. Morton-Finney had lived a full life, striving throughout his 108 years to always do more. (Endnote # 68)

George Burns was one of our centenarians. His death reminded us that you are never too old. He lost his true love and partner in comedy, Gracie Allen, in 1964, when he was 68. He already had a number of successful television, radio, and movie productions to his credit. He could have retired. Instead, he took on another TV series, played an ex-Vaudevillian in "The Sunshine Boys" and won an Academy Award at age 80. At 95, after four more successful movies, and a best seller, he hosted a TV special and won a Grammy. He refused to quit and we are all better for it. When his 100th birthday shows sold out a couple of years in advance, Burns said, "I can't die. I've got too much to lose. I'm booked." He did die. But it is the world that feels the loss. (Endnote # 69)

Martin E. Miller, Indiana's # 1 Advocate for Aging Services climbed the stairs leading to the Indiana State Capitol Building to attend a party to celebrate his 100th birthday held in the Statehouse Rotunda. Hundreds of people joined this public ceremony to recognize his valuable contributions to the State of Indiana and to this nation.

Curt Martindale of Little Cincinnati, Indiana and a long-time fan of Indiana University basketball received an I.U. cap from Coach Bob Knight on his 103nd birthday. During an interview just prior to his 103rd birthday, he was wearing the I.U. cap with pride. (Endnote # 70)

Robert Jackson of Baltimore, Maryland was a volunteer foster grandfather at age 102. When Jackson was a boy, his grandmother—a former slave—taught him that patience and good manners were the best way to cope with life in the segregated South. He's passing on the lessons he's learned about respect of others, trying to help incarcerated juvenile offenders straighten out their lives. Jackson uses kindness and gentle coaxing—not criticism—to teach his lessons in a slow, deliberate voice. He believes that young people today could stay out of trouble if they just showed some restraint and respect toward each other. That is what he tries to teach the youths at the Thomas Waxter Center where he began volunteering in 1981, at the age of 87. (Endnote # 71)

WHAT DO CENTENARIANS HAVE IN COMMON?

Surveys show that many centenarians are strong-minded and have confronted tough times. Humor is a great coping strategy. The authors believe an enthusiasm for life and living is also shared by most centenarians. And, they treasure their independence.

Leonard W. Poon, Director of the University of Georgia's Gerontology Center and head of the nation's biggest centenarian study says that there are several factors to take into consideration in determining the odds of living to age 100. Of course, genes count. Yet heredity is not all. You can have strong genes and die young for lack of a healthy diet, competent medical care or the ability to cope with stress. Good health habits matter. "That's the good news," Dr. Poon says. "We all have a chance of becoming centenarians." (Endnote # 72)

When centenarians were asked about their secret for living to be 100 years of age, the responses varied:

"I'd get old fast if I sat around doing nothing," **said Sidney Amber** who at age 108 worked as a maitre d' at a busy restaurant in San Francisco's famed Union Square. He was a customer at the restaurant and when the restaurant host failed to show up one day, he volunteered to do the job. When he finished for the day, the owner hired him to work four hours a day, three to four days a week. He seated at least 50 people an hour. (Endnote # 73)

"I credit the Good Lord for allowing me to live past the century mark, along with hard work," said Curt Martindale during an interview just prior to his 103rd birthday. "Hard work won't hurt anybody!" Curt said. (Endnote # 74)

During her 118th birthday party at the Florida Manor nursing facility in Orlando, Florida, Mary Thompson blew out the inferno of 118 candles on her cake—with a blow dryer. Mary was described as having a zest for living. At 118, she was very active, mentally alert, and strolls outside each day after breakfast. She said that "taking time to enjoy life is one of the secrets to her longevity. You should try to enjoy each day as it comes." (Endnote # 75)

Emma Winn, daughter of former slaves, died in 1994 at age 118. She accredited her longevity to greens, cornbread and "good hard work." She recalled some advice she got from her doctor when she was age 50. "He told me I'd kill myself if I kept up that pace," said Winn, who kept working for decades and outlived the doctor. (Endnote # 76)

During an interview with Rose Chestnut, age 102, she said that her secret to long life was going to church and hard work. (Endnote # 77)

Ethel Greenwood, age 100, attributes her longevity to "it runs in the family." Ethel's mother and great-great-grandfather lived to 100, one of her grandfathers lived to 105, and at the time of the interview two of her sisters were in their 90s. (Endnote # 78)

After 115 birthdays, Margaret Skeete, of Radford, Virginia still had her sense of humor and a craving for sweets. She was unimpressed by her longevity. "I guess that's something, but it doesn't buy me anything," she said, as a steady stream of friends stopped by her town house to celebrate her birthday. When asked for the secret to a long life, her daughter quipped, "Eat plenty of sweets." (Endnote # 79)

Friday, January 25, 1997 was celebrated as Maurice Wayman Evans Day in Bloomington, Indiana as Evans celebrated his 103rd Birthday. He enlisted in the Army during World War I and was a drill sergeant from 1917 to 1919. He settled back in Bloomington where he went into the barber business with his father. After retiring he became an avid volunteer around town. He was a leader at the Bethel African Methodist Church, a member of the American Legion, Area 10 Agency on Aging and the Older American Center. At age 103, he said he felt as young as ever. He shared his secret for a long, happy life: "Trust in the good Lord, help people and love everybody." (Endnote # 80)

Former math teacher Myrtle Mae Loy is 100 years of age, but she can still add up her grocery bill faster than the cashier can total it on the register. "Most of my former students are white-haired and bald headed. Why, they are in their 70's," she said. Her love of teaching lingers. Just two years ago, Loy took on a new student that was having trouble with a required college math class. "I got him through it so that he could go on," she said. Until she broke her hip at age 99, Loy plowed and planted the spacious garden behind her house and mowed the lawn when the grass grew high. She now hires out the plowing. Difficulty bending over does not keep her from weeding—she simply sits on the ground and scoots her way around. She lives alone, makes trips to the grocery store and bank, likes to cook and has a freezer stocked with garden overflow. "Following your interests is what matters," said Loy. (Endnote # 81)

And, what do the centenarians have in common with individuals age 60 to 100. Probably no more than individuals in any other age group that spans 40 plus years or, for that matter, individuals below the age of 60. Then why are they labeled by some as "Senior Citizens" or "Older Americans"? We do not refer to those individuals below age 60 as "Junior Citizens".

APPENDIX 1

This book is dedicated to our mother, Ruby Alice, and to the memory of our father, James Ivan. Because of them, we are. This and the following page contain the authors' favorite pictures of "Mother" and "Dad".

High School Picture of Ruby

Ivan with His "Catch" of the Day

Wedding Picture of Ruby Alice and James Ivan

Geneva Shedd-Wright and Charlotte Gore

APPENDIX 2

April 9, 1980

Dear Contributor:

Thank you for sending us your Viewpoint. I'm sorry to have
to tell you that we cannot use it.

Since we receive many Viewpoints daily, we cannot criticize
each one individually. But let me tell you ways in which
a perfectly sound idea can be wrong for us.

We may have a similar Viewpoint already scheduled. Or your
article may deal with very current events that will not be
of interest when our issue comes out several months from
now. Or it may be that the subject matter of your manuscript
is not appropriate for Glamour.

I'm sorry I cannot answer your letter personally, but I do
hope this letter helps you understand why we were unable to
accept your Viewpoint.

Again, thank you for your interest in Glamour.

Sincerely,

Katy Dobbs

Viewpoint Editor

PS. I'm sorry, but very few of our
readers are 90. This
topic is inappropriate for us.

Letter from well-known national fashion magazine

Geneva Shedd-Wright and Charlotte Gore

REFERENCES/ENDNOTES

ABOUT THE AUTHORS

1. The Indianapolis Star, The Indianapolis News, and the Herald Times (Bloomington, Indiana) Newspapers, March 24, 1996 through April 6, 1996.

PART ONE

2. The Indianapolis Star, The Indianapolis News, and the Herald Times (Bloomington, Indiana) Newspapers, March 24, 1996 through April 6, 1996.
3. Ibid.

PART TWO

4. Rob Goebel, "The Call of Duty," The Indianapolis Star Newspaper, November 11, 1993.
5. Ibid.
6. Ibid.
7. The Associated Press, "War Opened Hoosier's World," The Indianapolis News Newspaper, November 11, 1993.

8. Martin Merzer, "41 Tough, Crusty Paratroopers Re-Enact Their D-Day Jumps," The Indianapolis Star Newspaper, June 6, 1994.
9. Patrick McDowell, "Veterans Re-Enact Parachute Mission," The Herald Times (Bloomington, Indiana) Newspaper, June 6, 1994.
10. Martin Merzer, "41 Tough, Crusty Paratroopers Re-Enact Their D-Day Jumps," The Indianapolis Star Newspaper, June 6, 1994.
11. Ibid.
12. Associated Press, "Marines of Iwo Jima Have Reunion at Purdue," The Indianapolis Star Newspaper, June 22, 1996.
13. Richard D. Walton, "New Monument Fills Void for Former Servicewomen," The Indianapolis Star Newspaper, October 19, 1997.
14. Jackie Sheckler, "Bedford Man Happy To Be a Veteran of War and Life," The Herald Times (Bloomington, Indiana) Newspaper, April 3, 1996.
15. Kara L. Massey, "A Few Good Women Are Being Sought by WWII Marine," The Indianapolis Star Newspaper, January 2, 1997.
16. Matt Getts, "Niles Woman Honored for WWI Service to U.S. Troops," Senior Life Newspaper

published in South Bend, Indiana, November 1993.

17. Bill Hewitt, Cathy Nolan, and Jane Sugden, "Onto the Beach," page 36, People Magazine, May 30, 1994.

18. Sondra Farrell Bazrod, "WWI Veteran, 99, Takes a Look Back," page 2, Los Angeles Times, Valley Edition, June 23, 1994.

19. Barry Staver, "Forever Wilma," People Magazine, July 18, 1994.

20. Skip Hess, "Eagle-Eyed Observer Tracks Falcons from Downtown Perch," The Indianapolis Star Newspaper, June 30, 1996.

21. Gene D. Cohen, "Contemplating Creativity: You Can Do Things You Don't Know You can Do," AARP Bulletin, Vol. 38, No. 4, April 1997.

22. Susan L. Crowley, "Alfred Eisenstaedt's World View: Life's Premier Photographer Still Practicing his Craft," AARP Bulletin, October 1993.

23. James L. Patterson Jr., "Black Photographer Focuses on Life," The Indianapolis Star Newspaper, January 9, 1994.

24. Ramsey Campbell, "Grandma has Exotic Little Secret," The Indianapolis Star Newspaper, January 9, 1994.

25. Linda Feldman, "Salve for a Doctor's Own Pain," Los Angeles Times, June 21, 1994.
26. "Butterin' Up Garth," People Magazine, Fall 1994, Special Issue.
27. Sondra Farrell Bazrod, "Van Gets a Touch of Brass," Los Angeles Times, June 1, 1994.
28. "Lawn Day's Journey," People Magazine, September 12, 1994, Vol. 42, Issue 11, page 108.
29. Diana Kunde, "Seniors Find Fulfillment in Second Careers," The Indianapolis Star Newspaper, March 5, 1995.
30. Peter Key, "A Family Business," The Indianapolis Star Newspaper, February 4, 1996.
31. Connie Cass, "Exhibit Honors Workers with Decades on the Job," The Indianapolis Star Newspaper, September 9, 1995.
32. Annette Kondo, "Another Recipe for Investing Success," The Indianapolis Star Newspaper, February 17, 1996.
33. Associated Press, "Shuttle Aloft with Oldest Man in Space," The Herald Times (Bloomington, Indiana) Newspaper, November 20, 1996.
34. Christine Wicker, "Age Fails to Deter Determined Octogenarian with Dream," The Indianapolis Star Newspaper, May 4, 1996.

35. Associated Press, "At 87, Avon Lady Still Makes her Makeup Rounds," The Indianapolis Star Newspaper, November 9, 1997.

36. Diana Kunde, "Seniors Find Fulfillment in Second Careers," The Indianapolis Star Newspaper, March 5, 1995.

37. Donna S. Mullinix, "Bulldog Settles Out of Court and into Retirement," The Indianapolis Star Newspaper, January 16, 1994.

38. Kimberly Murphy, Associated Press, "Jobs Program Helps Old Hands Stay Productive Longer," Los Angeles Times, July 10, 1994.

39. Linda Feldman, "Bringing Vitality to the Topic of Death," Los Angeles Times, July 17, 1994.

40. Paul Dean, "At the Fore Once Again," Los Angeles Times, July 17, 1994.

41. Roy Rivenburg, "An Invented Life," Los Angeles Times, June 19, 1994.

42. Bill Vogren, Associated Press, "Cast-off Crockery is Just What They're Looking For," Los Angeles Times, July 10, 1994.

43. Bob Sipchen, "A Man of the Woods," Los Angeles Times, July 24, 1994.

44. Michael Forrest, "The King of the Rock," Home Edition, Los Angeles Times, July 24, 1994, page 6.

45. Susan Paterno, "A Career of Caring for Kids," Los Angeles Times, July 31, 1994.
46. Janice Min and Amy Roffmann New, "Out of This World," People Magazine, Vol. 42, Issue 3, July 18, 1994, page 74.
47. Deborah Mendez, "Fascination With Storms Spawned a Career," Los Angeles Times, July 1, 1995.
48. "A Bad Ewe-Turn," People Magazine, July 18, 1994, Vol. 42, Issue 3, page 47.
49. Linda Feldman, "Singing With One Voice," Los Angeles Times, May 8, 1994.
50. Sue Reilly, "Plucky Banker Goes Through Life with a Banjo," Los Angeles Times, June 27, 1994.
51. Mark Sabbatini, "Trading Post Offers More Than Just Bargains," Los Angeles Times, June 27, 1994.
52. Linda Feldman, "Passionate About His Profession," Los Angeles Times, January 1, 1995.
53. Ken Dychtwald, Ph.D. and Joe Flower, "Age Wave: The Challenges and Opportunities of an Aging America," A Bantam Books, 1990.
54. Bob Moseley, "Youth vs. Experience," Tennis USTA, Supplement to Tennis Magazine, August 1998.

55. Mary Huzinec, "The Wish to Fish," People Magazine, July 18, 1994, Vol. 42, Issue 3, page 41.
56. Donna S. Mullinix, "Free Wheeling," The Indianapolis Star, July 10, 1998.
57. Paula Story, "Dribbling Grannies Hold Court," The Indianapolis Star, October 30, 1997.
58. Ann Landers, "81-Year-Old Finds Herself in Touchy Situation," Los Angeles Times, August 7, 1994.
59. Associated Press, "At 87, Illinois Runner Leaves Her Colleagues' Records in the Dust," The Indianapolis Star, July 21, 1996.
60. Sean O'Brien, "91-Year-Old Cyclist Keeps Rolling in Hilly," The Herald Times (Bloomington, Indiana), October 19, 1997.
61. Daniel Q. Haney, "Working Out, Pumping Up Give Elderly a Lift, Study Finds," Indianapolis Star, July 10, 1994.
62. Paul Lambert and Anne Maier, "Mommie Oldest," People Magazine, November 21, 1994, Vol. 42, Issue 21, page 78.

PART THREE

63. Caryl Stern, "What We Can Lean From People Who Live to 100!" The Indianapolis Star

Parade Sunday Newspaper Magazine, January 21, 1996.

64. Ibid.
65. Ibid.
66. Ibid.
67. Ibid.
68. Crystal Livers-Powers, "Black Lawyer, 106, Gives Advice That Never Gets Old, The Indianapolis Star Newspaper, March 1, 1996.
69. Editorial, "In Death, Burns Offers Lessons," The Herald Times (Bloomington, Indiana) Newspaper, March 14, 1996.
70. Claude Parsons, "Curt Martindale is Nearing his 103rd Birthday," The Times-Mail Prime Advantage (Little Cincinnati, Indiana), February 17, 1994.
71. Associated Press, "Centenarian Provides Role Model for Getting Along," The Indianapolis Star Newspaper, December 6, 1996.
72. Caryl Stern, "What We Can Learn From People Who Live to 100!" The Indianapolis Star Parade Sunday Newspaper Magazine, January 21, 1996
73. Susan Krajewski, "108-Year-Old Still Works as a Maitre d'!," National Enquirer, April 1994.
74. Claude Parsons, "Curt Martindale is Nearing his 103rd Birthday," The Times-Mail Prime

Advantage (Little Cincinnati, Indiana), February 17, 1994.

75. Dan McDonald, "Happy 118th, Mary!" National Enquirer, April 1994.

76. Associated Press, "Emma Winn, 118 Year-Old Daughter of Slaves, Dies," The Herald Times (Bloomington, Indiana) Newspaper, April 9, 1994.

77. Dann Denny, "Living Past the Century Mark," Sunday Herald Times (Bloomington, Indiana) Newspaper, March 27, 1994.

78. Ibid.

79. "After All Those Years," The Indianapolis Star Newspaper, October 30, 1993.

80. Jennifer Jill Fowler, "Evans Marks 103rd Birthday," Herald Times (Bloomington, Indiana) Newspaper, January 25, 1997.

81. Laura Lane, "100 Years and Counting," The College, published by Indiana University Alumni Association in Cooperation with the College of Arts & Sciences Alumni Association, Spring 1997, Volume 20, No. 2.

BE INCLUDED IN OUR NEXT PUBLICATION:

Would you, a friend, or relative like to be included in future publication(s) of "From the Hills of Indiana to the Shores of California"? If yes, complete the form on the next page and include the signature releases required. If you want to include a photograph, complete the additional part of the form. Photographs should include only the person whose life experience is provided. Copies may be made of the form if more than one submission is desired. Send submissions to: **P.O. Box 1547, Nashville, IN 47448**.

We cannot guarantee your life experience will be included in future publications, however, all submissions will be carefully reviewed and considered. Please, also note, that if your life experience is used, street addresses will not be included.

We are sorry, but we are not able to return submissions.

Sincerely,

Geneva Shedd-Wright and Charlotte Gore

RELEASE:

I do hereby authorize the authors/publishers of "From the Hills of Indiana to the Shores of California" and or parties designated by the publishers to use my life experience and/or my name and/or my photograph for purposes of reproduction in future publications (enclose copy of submission). You agree that we may edit/publish the material in whole or part. You also represent that the information provided is true and accurate to the best of your knowledge and you agree to indemnify and hold us harmless for any claims made against us for the use of your materials.

Signature:_____

Name: _____

Age: _____

Street
Address:_____

City: _____

State: _____ Zip Code:_____

Additional release signature(s) are required if photographs are included for publication. See the next page.

PHOTOGRAPH USE RELEASE:

I do hereby authorize the publishers of "From the Hills of Indiana to the Shores of California" and or parties designated by the publishers to use my photograph of_____
for purposes of reproduction in a future publication(s). I represent that I am the owner of said photograph and that I have legal power to consent to its publication.

Photographer's Signature:

_____

Street Address:

_____

City: _____

State:_____   Zip Code:_____